Everyday Vegetarian
Delicious Meatless Brea...
Recipes You Can Make in Minutes!

by **Vesela Tabakova**
Text copyright(c)2013 Vesela Tabakova

Table Of Contents

What's For Dinner?

If I have to be honest, vegetarian meals are my personal favorites and I can happily live without meat at all. However, because I have to cook for a large family and my husband is a big meat lover, I always serve both vegetarian as well as meat dishes for those who like it.

This cookbook is a collection of my family's favorite vegetarian recipes - easy to make and always delicious. They can be served on their own or as side dishes with some meat. If you're looking for quick, healthy and nutritious meal ideas for your family, you may want to try some of our favorite vegetarian recipes.

Salads and Appetizers

Summer Macaroni Salad

Serves 6

Ingredients:

2 cups macaroni pasta

2 hard boiled eggs, chopped

2 roasted red bell peppers, thinly sliced

3 tbsp fresh dill, chopped

3-4 spring onions, finely cut

1/3 cup mayonnaise

2 tbsp lemon juice

freshly ground black pepper, to taste

Directions:

Cook macaroni as directed on package. When cooked through but still slightly firm remove from heat, drain and rinse with cool water.

Put chopped onions into a salad bowl and toss with the lemon juice. Add in macaroni and all the other ingredients. Season with salt and pepper to taste and serve.

Traditional Greek Salad

Serves 6

Ingredients:

2 cucumbers, diced

2 tomatoes, sliced

1 green lettuce, cut in thin strips

2 red bell peppers, cut

1/2 cup black olives, pitted

3.5 oz feta cheese, cut

1 red onion, sliced

2 tbsp olive oil

2 tbsp lemon juice

salt and ground black pepper, to taste

Directions:

Dice the cucumbers and slice the tomatoes. Tear the lettuce or cut it in thin strips. De-seed and cut the peppers in strips.

Combine all vegetables in a salad bowl. Add the olives and the feta cheese cut in cubes.

In a small cup stir the olive oil and the lemon juice with salt and pepper. Pour over the salad and stir again.

Apple, Celery and Walnut Salad

Serves 4

Ingredients:

4 apples, quartered, cores removed, thinly sliced

1 celery rib, thinly sliced

1/2 cup walnuts, chopped

2 tbsp raisins

1 large red onion, thinly sliced

3 tbsp apple cider vinegar

2 tbsp sunflower oil

Directions:

Combine vinegar, oil, salt and pepper in a small bowl. Whisk until well combined.

Combine apples, celery, walnuts, raisins and onion in a large bowl. Drizzle with dressing and toss gently to combine.

Italian Caprese Salad

Serves 6

Ingredients:

4 tomatoes, sliced

6 oz mozzarella cheese, sliced

10 fresh basil leaves

3 tbsp olive oil

2 tbsp red wine vinegar

salt, to taste

Directions:

Slice the tomatoes and mozzarella, then layer the tomato slices, whole fresh basil leaves and mozzarella slices on a plate.

Drizzle olive oil and vinegar over the salad and serve.

Beet and Bean Sprout Salad

Serves 4

Ingredients:

7 beet greens, finely sliced

2 medium tomatoes, cut into wedges

1 cup bean sprouts, washed

1 tbsp grated lemon rind

2 garlic cloves, crushed

1/2 cup lemon juice

4 tbsp olive oil

1/2 tsp salt

Directions:

In a large bowl toss together beet greens, bean sprouts and tomatoes.

Prepare a dressing from the oil, lemon juice, lemon rind, salt and garlic and pour it over the salad.

Refrigerate for 2 hours to allow the flavor to develop before serving. Serve chilled.

Asian Coleslaw

Serves 4

Ingredients:

for the salad

1/2 Chinese cabbage, shredded

1 green bell pepper, sliced into thin strips

1 carrot, cut into thin strips

4 spring onions, chopped

for the dressing

3 tbsp lemon juice

3 tbsp soy sauce

3 tbsp sweet chilly sauce

Directions:

Remove any damaged outer leaves and rinse cabbage. Holding cabbage from the base and, starting at the opposite end, shred leaves thinly.

Combine vegetables first then dressing ingredients. Pour over salad and toss well.

Baby Spinach Salad

Serves 4

Ingredients:

1 bag baby spinach, washed and dried

9 oz feta cheese, coarsely crumbled

1 red bell pepper, cut in slices

1 cup cherry tomatoes, halved

1 red onion, finely chopped

1 cup black olives, pitted

1 tsp dried oregano

1 large garlic clove

3 tbsp red wine vinegar

4 tbsp olive oil

salt and freshly ground black pepper to taste

Directions:

Prepare the dressing by blending the garlic and the oregano with the olive oil and the vinegar in a food processor.

Place the spinach leaves in a large salad bowl and toss with the dressing. Add the rest of the ingredients and give everything a toss again. Season to taste with black pepper and salt.

Tabbouleh

Serves 6

Ingredients:

1 cup raw bulgur

2 cups boiling water

a bunch of parsley, finely cut

2 tomatoes, chopped

3 tbsp olive oil

2 garlic cloves, minced

6-7 spring onions, chopped

10 fresh mint leaves, chopped

juice of two lemons

salt and black pepper, to taste

Directions:

Bring water and salt to a boil, then pour over bulgur. Cover and set aside for 15 minutes to steam. Drain excess water from bulgur and fluff with a fork. Leave to chill.

In a large bowl, mix together the parsley, tomatoes, olive oil, garlic, spring onions and mint. Stir in the cooled bulgur and season to taste with salt, pepper, and lemon juice.

Fatoush

Serves 6

Ingredients:

2 cups lettuce, washed, dried, and chopped

3 tomatoes, chopped

1 cucumber, peeled and chopped

1 green pepper, deseeded and chopped

1 cup radishes, sliced in half

1 small red onion, finely chopped

half a bunch of parsley, finely cut

2 tbsp finely chopped fresh mint

3 tbsp olive oil

4 tbsp lemon juice

salt and black pepper, to taste

2 whole-wheat pita breads

Directions:

Toast the pita breads in a skillet until they are browned and crisp. Set aside.

Place the lettuce, tomatoes, cucumbers, green pepper, radishes, onion, parsley and mint in a salad bowl. Break up the toasted pita into bite-size pieces and add to the salad.

Prepare the dressing by whisking together the olive oil with the lemon juice, a pinch of salt and some black pepper. Pour it over the salad and toss to combine.

The Best Orzo Salad

Serves 6

Ingredients:

for the dressing:

1/3 cup olive oil

3/4 cup fresh lemon juice

1 tbsp dried mint

for the salad:

1 cup uncooked orzo

2 tbsp olive oil

a bunch of spring onions, chopped

3 green peppers, diced

1/2 cup black olives, pitted, cut

2 tomatoes, diced

1 cup raw sunflower seeds

Directions:

The dressing: Combine olive oil, lemon juice, and mint in a small bowl, mixing well. Place the dressing in the refrigerator until ready to use.

Cook the orzo according to package directions (in salted water) and rinse thoroughly with cold water when you strain it. Transfer to a large bowl and toss with the olive oil. Allow orzo to cool completely.

Once orzo is cooled, add the diced peppers, finely cut spring onions, olives and diced tomatoes stirring until mixed well.

the salad, tossing to evenly coat. Add salt and pepper to taste and sprinkle with sunflower seeds.

Chickpea Salad with Cucumbers, Peppers and Tomatoes

Serves 4

Ingredients:

1 cup canned chickpeas, drained and rinsed

2 spring onions, thinly sliced

1 small cucumber, diced

2 green bell peppers, chopped

2 tomatoes, diced

2 tbsp chopped fresh parsley

1 tsp capers, drained and rinsed

juice of half lemon

2 tbsp sunflower oil

1 tbsp red wine vinegar

salt and pepper, to taste

a pinch of dried oregano

Directions:

In a medium bowl toss together the chickpeas, spring onions, cucumber, bell pepper, tomato, parsley, capers, and lemon juice.

In a smaller bowl stir together the remaining ingredients and pour over the chickpea salad. Toss well to coat and allow to marinate, stirring occasionally, for at least one hour before serving.

Green Lettuce Salad

Serves 4

Ingredients:

1 green lettuce, washed and drained

1 cucumber

a bunch of radishes

a bunch of spring onions

the juice of half a lemon or 2 tbsp of white wine vinegar

3 tbsp sunflower or olive oil

salt, to taste

Directions:

Cut the lettuce into thin strips. Slice the cucumber and the radishes as thinly as possible and chop the spring onions.

Mix all the salad ingredients in a large bowl, add the lemon juice and oil and season with salt to taste.

Fried Zucchinis with Homemade Tomato Sauce

Serves 4

Ingredients:

4 zucchinis medium size

1 cup all purpose flour

2 cups sunflower oil for frying

salt, to taste

for the tomato sauce

4-5 ripe tomatoes, skinned and grated

1 carrot

1/2 onion

2 cloves garlic, whole

1/2 tsp salt

1/2 sunflower oil

1 tsp sugar

3 tbsp flour

1/2 bunch fresh parsley

Directions:

Wash and peel the zucchinis, and cut them in thin diagonal slices or in rings 1/4 inch thick. Salt and leave them in a suitable bowl placing it inclined to drain away the juices.

Coat the zucchinis with flour, then fry turning on both sides until they are golden-brown (about 3 minutes on each side). Transfer to paper towels and pat dry.

Heat the oil in a large skillet and cook the onion and the carrot until soft. Add the grated tomatoes together with two whole garlic cloves. Season with salt and a tsp of sugar. Simmer in low heat until thick and ready. Sprinkle with parsley and pour over the fried zucchinis.

Simple Potato Salad

Serves 5-6

Ingredients:

4-5 large potatoes

2-3 spring onions, finely chopped

juice of half a lemon

1/4 cup sunflower or olive oil

salt and pepper, to taste

fresh parsley, to serve

Directions:

Peel and boil the potatoes for about 20-25 minutes, drain and leave to cool.

In a salad bowl add the finely chopped spring onions, the lemon juice, salt, pepper and olive oil, and mix gently. Cut the potatoes into cubes and add to the salad bowl. Gently mix, sprinkle with parsley. Serve cold.

Cabbage, Carrot and Turnip Salad

Serves 4

Ingredients:

9 oz fresh white cabbage, shredded

9 oz carrots, shredded

9 oz white turnips, shredded

1/2 a bunch of parsley

2 tbsp white vinegar

3 tbsp sunflower oil

salt, to taste

Directions:

Combine vegetables in a large bowl and mix well. Add salt, vinegar and oil. Stir and sprinkle with parsley.

Red Cabbage Salad

Serves 6

Ingredients:

1 small head red cabbage, cored and chopped

a bunch of fresh dill, finely cut

3 tbsp sunflower oil

3 tbsp red wine vinegar

1 tbsp white sugar

1 tsp salt

black pepper, to taste

Directions:

In a small bowl, mix the oil, red wine vinegar, sugar and black pepper.

Place the cabbage in a large salad bowl. Sprinkle the salt on top and crunch it with your hands to soften.

Pour dressing over the cabbage, and toss to coat. Sprinkle the salad with dill, cover it with foil and leave it in the refrigerator for half an hour before serving.

Simple Okra Salad

Serves 4

Ingredients:

1 lb young okras

juice from 1 lemon

1/2 bunch of parsley, chopped

2 hard tomatoes

3 tbsp sunflower oil

1/2 tsp black pepper

salt, to taste

Directions:

Trim okras, wash and cook in salted water. Drain and cool when tender.

In a small bowl mix well the lemon juice and sunflower oil, salt and pepper.

Pour the dressing over the okras and sprinkle with chopped parsley. Wash tomatoes and cut them into slices, then garnish the salad with them.

Lazy Cucumber Salad

Serves 4

Ingredients:

2 medium cucumbers, sliced

a bunch of fresh dill

2 cloves garlic

3 tbsp white vinegar

5 tbsp olive oil

salt, to taste

Directions:

Cut the cucumbers in rings and put them on a plate. Add the finely cut dill, the pressed garlic and season with salt, vinegar and oil. Mix well and serve cold.

Spring Beetroot Salad

Serves 4

Ingredients:

2-3 small beets, peeled

3 spring onions, chopped

3 garlic cloves, pressed

2 tbsp red wine vinegar

2-3 tbsp sunflower oil

salt, to taste

Directions:

Place the beets in a steam basket set over a pot of boiling water. Steam for about 15 - 20 minutes, or until tender. Leave to cool.

Grate the beets and put them in a salad bowl. Add the crushed garlic cloves, the finely cut spring onions and mix well. Season with salt, vinegar and sunflower oil.

Tomato Couscous Salad

Serves 2

Ingredients:

1 cup medium couscous

1 cup hot water

2 ripe tomatoes, diced

1/2 red onion, finely cut

5 tbsp sunflower oil

4 tbsp lemon juice

1 tbsp dry mint

Directions:

Place the couscous in a large bowl. Boil water with one tablespoon of olive oil and pour over the couscous. Cover and set aside for 10 minutes. Fluff couscous with a fork and when it is completely cold, stir in the tomatoes, onion and dry mint.

In a separate small bowl, combine the remaining olive oil, the lemon juice and salt, add to the couscous and stir until well combined.

Garlicky Carrot Salad

Serves 4

Ingredients:

4 carrots, shredded

1 apple, peeled, cored and shredded

2 garlic cloves, crushed

2 tbsp lemon juice

2 tbsp honey

salt and pepper, to taste

Directions:

In a bowl, combine the shredded carrots, apple, lemon juice, honey, garlic, salt and pepper. Toss and chill before serving.

Roasted Eggplant and Pepper Salad

Serves 4

Ingredients:

2 medium eggplants

2 red or green bell peppers

2 tomatoes

3 cloves garlic, crushed

fresh parsley

1-2 tbsp red wine vinegar

olive oil, as needed

salt, pepper

Directions:

Wash and dry the vegetables. Prick the skin of the eggplants. Bake the eggplants, tomatoes and peppers in a pre-heated oven at 480 F for about 40 minutes, until the skins are well burnt. Take out of the oven and leave in a covered container for about 10 minutes.

Peel the skins off and drain well the extra juices. De-seed the peppers. Cut all the vegetables into very small pieces or cut in a blender.

Add the garlic and stir well. Add the olive oil, vinegar and salt to taste. Stir again. Serve sprinkled with parsley.

Green Bean Salad

Serves 6

Ingredients:

2 cups green beans, cooked

1 onion, sliced

4 garlic cloves, crushed

1 tbsp fresh mint, chopped

1 bunch of fresh dill, finely chopped

3 tbsp olive oil

1 tablespoon apple cider vinegar

salt and pepper, to taste

Directions:

Pour the green beans in a medium bowl, and mix with onion, mint and dill.

In a smaller bowl combine olive oil, vinegar, garlic, salt, and pepper. Toss into the green bean mixture.

Zucchini Pasta Salad

Serves 6

Ingredients:

2 cups spiral pasta

2 zucchinis, sliced and halved

4 tomatoes, cut

1 cup white mushrooms, cut

1 small red onion, chopped

2 tbsp fresh basil leaves, chopped

3.5 oz blue cheese

2 tbsp sunflower oil

1 tbsp lemon juice

black pepper, to taste

Directions:

Cook pasta according to directions or until al dente. Drain, rinse with cold water and drain again.

Place zucchinis, tomatoes, mushrooms and onion in a large bowl. Add pasta and mix gently.

Combine oil, lemon juice, basil, blue cheese and black pepper in a blender. Pour over salad. Toss gently and serve.

Russian Salad

Serves 6

Ingredients:

3 potatoes, boiled, cut

2 carrots, boiled, cut

1 cup canned green peas, drained

1 cup mayonnaise

5 pickled gherkins, chopped

black olives, to serve

salt, to taste

Directions:

Boil the potatoes and carrots, then chop into small cubes. Put everything, except for the mayonnaise, in a serving bowl and mix.

Add salt to taste, then stir in the mayonnaise. Garnish with parsley and olives. Serve cold.

Buckwheat Salad with Asparagus and Roasted Peppers

Serves 4-5

Ingredients:

1 cup buckwheat groats

1 3/4 cups vegetable broth

1/2 lb asparagus, trimmed and cut into 1 inch pieces

4 roasted red bell peppers, diced

2-3 spring onions, finely chopped

2 garlic cloves, crushed

1 tbsp red wine vinegar

3 tbsp olive oil

salt and black pepper, to taste

1/2 cup fresh parsley leaves, finely cut

Directions:

Heat a large dry saucepan and toast the buckwheat for about three minutes. Boil the vegetable broth and add it carefully to the buckwheat. Cover, reduce heat and simmer until buckwheat is tender and all liquid is absorbed (5-7 minutes). Remove from heat, fluff with a fork and set aside to cool.

Rinse out the saucepan and then bring about an inch of water to a boil. Cook the asparagus in a steamer basket or colander, 2 to 3 minutes until tender. Transfer the asparagus in a large bowl along with the roasted peppers. Add in the spring onions, garlic, red wine vinegar, salt, pepper and olive oil. Stir to combine. Add the buckwheat to the vegetable mixture. Sprinkle with parsley and toss the salad gently. Serve at room temperature.

Roasted Broccoli Buckwheat Salad

Serves 4-5

Ingredients:

1 cup buckwheat groats

1 3/4 cups water

1 head of broccoli, cut into small pieces

1 lb asparagus, trimmed and cut into 1 inch pieces

1/2 cup roasted cashews

1/2 cup basil leaves, minced

1/2 cup olive oil

2 garlic cloves, crushed

1/2 tsp salt

3 tbsp Parmesan cheese, grated, to serve

Directions:

Arrange vegetables on a baking sheet and drizzle with olive oil. Roast in a preheated to 350 F oven for about fifteen minutes or until tender.

Heat a large, dry saucepan and toast the buckwheat for about three minutes, or until it releases a nutty aroma. Boil the water and add it carefully to the buckwheat. Cover, reduce heat and simmer until buckwheat is tender and all liquid is absorbed (5-7 minutes). Remove from heat, fluff with a fork and set aside to cool.

Prepare the dressing by blending basil leaves, olive oil, garlic, and salt.

Toss vegetables, buckwheat and dressing together in a salad bowl. Add in cashews and serve sprinkled with Parmesan cheese.

Roasted Vegetable Quinoa Salad

Serves 6

Ingredients:

2 zucchinis, cut into bite sized pieces

1 eggplant cut into bite sized pieces

3 roasted red pepper, cut into bite sized pieces

4-5 small white mushrooms, whole

1 cup quinoa

4 sunflower oil

3 tbsp olive oil

1 tbsp apple cider vinegar

½ tsp summer savory or oregano

salt and pepper, to taste

7 oz feta, crumbled

Directions:

Toss the zucchinis, mushrooms and eggplant in the sunflower oil, salt and pepper. Place onto a baking sheet in a single layer and bake in a preheated 350 F oven for 30 minutes, flipping once.

Wash well, strain and cook the quinoa following package directions. Prepare the dressing from the olive oil, apple cider vinegar, savory, salt and pepper.

In a big bowl combine quinoa, roasted zucchinis, eggplant, mushrooms, roasted red peppers and feta. Toss the dressing into the salad.

Quinoa and Asparagus Salad

Serves 6

Ingredients:

1 cup quinoa, rinsed

2 cups water

8-9 spears of asparagus, woody ends trimmed, cut

2 bell peppers, deseeded, chopped

5.5 oz feta cheese, crumbled

¼ cup raw sunflower seeds

4 spring onions, chopped

2 tbsp fresh parsley, finely cut

2 tbsp lemon juice

1 tbsp honey

2 tbsp olive oil

1 tsp paprika

Directions:

Rinse quinoa very well in a fine mesh strainer under running water; set aside to drain. Place water and quinoa in a large saucepan over medium-high heat. Bring to the boil then reduce heat to low. Simmer for 15 minutes or until just tender. Set aside, covered, for 10 minutes.

Preheat an electric grill or grill pan and cook the asparagus for 2-3 minutes or until tender crisp.

Combine the asparagus, bell pepper, feta, sunflower seeds, spring onions and parsley with the quinoa.

Whisk the lemon juice, honey, oil and paprika in a small bowl until well combined. Add the dressing to the quinoa mixture. Season with pepper and toss to combine.

Fresh Mushroom Quinoa Salad

Serves 6

Ingredients:

½ cup quinoa

1 cup water

6 white mushrooms, sliced

1 cup cherry tomatoes, halved

¼ cup walnuts, chopped

½ bunch fresh parsley, finely cut

3-4 spring onions, finely cut

½ cup black olives, pitted and halved

For the dressing:

2 tbsp orange juice

1 tbsp apple cider vinegar

2 small garlic cloves, minced

2 tbsp olive oil

freshly ground black pepper, to taste

Directions:

Wash and cook the quinoa in the water. Cover and allow to cool for 10 minutes.

Combine mushrooms, tomatoes, onions, olives, parsley and walnuts in a large bowl. Add the cooled quinoa.

Whisk together the dressing ingredients and drizzle over the salad just before serving.

Quinoa an   k Bean Salad

Serves 5-6

Ingredients:

1 cup quinoa

2 cups water

1 cup black beans, cooked, rinsed and drained

½ cup sweet corn, cooked

1 red bell pepper, deseeded and chopped

4 spring onions, chopped

1 garlic clove, crushed

1 tbsp dry mint

2 tbsp lemon juice

½ tsp salt

1 tbsp apple cider vinegar

4 tbsp cup sunflower oil

Directions:

Rinse quinoa in a fine sieve under cold running water until water runs clear. Put quinoa in a pot with 2 cups of water. Bring to a boil, then reduce heat, cover and simmer for 15 minutes or until water is absorbed and quinoa is tender. Fluff quinoa with a fork and set aside to cool.

Put beans, corn, bell pepper, spring onions and garlic in a bowl and toss with vinegar, and black pepper to taste. Add quinoa and toss well again.

In a separate bowl whisk together lemon juice, salt and sunflower oil and drizzle over salad. Toss well and serve.

Cucumber Quinoa Salad

Serves 5-6

Ingredients:

1 cup quinoa, rinsed

2 cups water

1 large cucumber, diced

½ cup black olives, pitted

2 tbsp lemon juice

2 tbsp olive oil

1 bunch fresh dill, finely cut

Directions:

Wash quinoa very well in a fine mesh strainer under running water and set aside to drain. Place quinoa and 2 cups of cold water in a saucepan over high heat and bring to the boil. Reduce heat to low and simmer for 15 minutes. Set aside, covered, for 10 minutes, then transfer to a large bowl.

Add finely cut dill, cucumber and olives. Prepare a dressing with the lemon juice, olive oil, salt and pepper. Add it to the salad and toss to combine.

Soups

Rich Vegetable Soup

Serves 6

Ingredients:

½ cup quinoa

1 onion, chopped

1 potato, diced

1 carrot, diced

1 red bell pepper, chopped

2 tomatoes, chopped

1 zucchini, diced

1 tsp paprika

1 tsp savory

3-4 tbsp olive oil

black pepper, to taste

4 cups water

Directions:

Rinse quinoa very well in a fine mesh strainer under running water; set aside to drain.

Heat the oil in a large soup pot and gently sauté the onions and carrot for 2-3 minutes stirring every now and then. Add paprika, savory, potato, bell pepper, tomatoes and water. Stir to combine.

Cover, bring to a boil then lower heat and simmer for 10 minutes. Add in the quinoa and zucchini; cover and simmer for 15 minutes or until the vegetables are tender. Add in the lemon juice; stir to combine.

Winter Lentil Soup

Serves:10

Ingredients:

2 cups brown lentils

2 onions, chopped

5-6 cloves garlic, peeled

3 medium carrots, chopped

2-3 medium tomatoes, ripe

5-6 cups of water

4 tbsp olive oil

1 1/2 tsp paprika

1 tsp summer savory

Directions:

Heat the oil in a cooking pot, add the onions and carrots and sauté until golden. Add the paprika and washed lentils with 3-4 cups of warm water; continue to simmer.

Chop tomatoes and add them to the soup about 15 min after the lentils have started to simmer. Add savory and peeled garlic cloves. Let the soup simmer until the lentils are soft. Salt to taste.

Moroccan Lentil Soup

Serves 5-6

Ingredients:

1 cup red lentils

1 cup canned chickpeas, drained

2 onions, chopped

2 cloves garlic, minced

1 can chopped tomatoes

1 can white beans

3 carrots, diced

3 celery ribs, diced

4 cups water

1 tsp ginger, grated

1 tsp ground cardamom

1/2 tsp ground cumin

3 tbsp olive oil

Directions:

In large pot, sauté onions, garlic and ginger in olive oil for about 5 minutes. Add the water, lentils, chickpeas, white beans, tomatoes, carrots, celery, cardamom and cumin.

Bring to a boil for a few minutes then simmer for 1/2 hour or longer, until the lentils are tender.

Puree half the soup in a food processor or blender. Return the pureed soup to the pot, stir and serve.

Bean and Pasta Soup

Serves 6-7

Ingredients:

1 cup small pasta, cooked

1 can white beans, rinsed and drained

2 medium carrots, cut

1 cup fresh spinach , torn

1 medium onion, chopped

1 celery rib, chopped

2 garlic cloves, crushed

2 cups water

1 can tomatoes, diced and undrained

1 cup vegetable broth

1/2 tsp rosemary

1/2 tsp basil

3 tbsp olive oil

salt and pepper to taste

Directions:

Heat the olive oil over medium heat and sauté the onion, carrots and celery. Add the garlic and cook for a minute longer. Stir in the water, tomatoes, vegetable broth, basil, rosemary, salt and pepper.

Bring to a boil then reduce heat and simmer for 10 minutes or until the carrots are tender. Drain pasta and add it to the vegetables. Add the beans and spinach and cook until spinach is wilted.

White Bean Soup

Serves 6

Ingredients:

1 cup white beans

3 cups water

2-3 carrots

2 onions, finely chopped

1-2 tomatoes, grated

1 red bell pepper, chopped

4-5 springs of fresh mint and parsley

1 tsp paprika

3 tbsp sunflower oil

Directions:

Soak the beans in cold water for 3-4 hours, drain and discard the water.

Cover the beans with cold water. Add the oil, finely chopped carrots, onions and pepper.

Bring to the boil and simmer until the beans are tender. Add the grated tomatoes, mint, paprika and salt. Simmer for another 15 minutes.

Serve sprinkled with finely chopped parsley.

Creamy Zucchini Soup

Serves 4

Ingredients:

1 onion, finely chopped

2 garlic cloves, crushed

1 cup vegetable broth

1 cup water

5 zucchinis, peeled, thinly sliced

1 big potato, chopped

1/4 cup fresh basil leaves

1 tsp sugar

1/2 cup yogurt, to serve

Parmesan cheese, to serve

Directions:

Heat oil in a saucepan over medium heat and sauté the onion and garlic, stirring, for 2-3 minutes or until soft.

Add vegetable broth and water and bring to the boil then reduce heat to medium low. Add zucchinis, the potato, a tsp of sugar, and simmer, stirring occasionally, for 10 minutes or until the zucchinis are soft. Add basil and simmer for 2-3 minutes.

Set aside to cool then blend in batches and reheat soup. Serve with a dollop of yogurt and/or sprinkled with Parmesan cheese.

Broccoli, Zucchini and Blue Cheese Soup

Serves 6

Ingredients:

2 leeks, white part only, sliced

1 head broccoli, coarsely chopped

2 zucchinis, chopped

1 potato, chopped

2 cups vegetable broth

2 cups water

3 tbsp olive oil

3.5 oz blue cheese, crumbled

1/3 cup light cream

Directions:

Heat the oil in a large saucepan over medium heat. Sauté the leeks, stirring, for 5 minutes or until soft. Add bite sized pieces of broccoli, zucchinis, potato, water and broth and bring to a boil.

Reduce heat to low and simmer, stirring occasionally, for 10 minutes or until vegetables are just tender. Remove from heat and set aside for 5 minutes to cool slightly.

Transfer soup to a blender. Add the cheese and blend in batches until smooth. Return to saucepan and place over low heat. Add cream and stir to combine. Season with salt and pepper to taste.

Beetroot and Carrot Soup

Serves 6

Ingredients:

4 beets, washed and peeled

2 carrots, peeled, chopped

2 potatoes, peeled, chopped

1 medium onion, chopped

2 cups vegetable broth

2 cups water

2 tbsp yogurt

2 tbsp olive oil

a bunch or spring onions, cut, to serve

Directions:

Peel and chop the beets. Heat olive oil in a saucepan over medium high heat and sauté onion and carrot until onion is tender. Add beets, potatoes, broth and water.

Bring to the boil. Reduce heat to medium and simmer, partially covered, for 30 - 40 minutes or until beets are tender. Cool slightly.

Blend soup in batches, until smooth. Return it to pan over low heat and cook, stirring, for 4 to 5 minutes or until heated through. Season with salt and pepper. Serve soup topped with yogurt and sprinkled with spring onions.

Borscht

Serves 6

Ingredients:

4 beets, peeled, quartered

1 carrot, peeled, chopped

1 parsnip, peeled, cut into chunks

1 leek, white part only, sliced

1 onion, chopped

1/3 cup lemon juice

1/2 tsp nutmeg

3 bay leaves

6 cups vegetable broth

1 cup sour cream

2-3 dill springs, chopped

Directions:

Place the beets, carrot, parsnip, leek, onion, lemon juice, spices and bay leaves in a large saucepan with the vegetable broth.

Bring to the boil, then reduce the heat to low and simmer, partially covered, for 1 1/2 hours. Cool slightly, then blend in batches and season well with salt and pepper.

Return to saucepan and gently heat through. Place in bowls and garnish with sour cream and dill.

Curried Parsnip Soup

Serves 6

Ingredients:

1.5 lb parsnips, peeled, chopped

2 onions, chopped

2 garlic cloves, cut

3 tbsp olive oil

1 tbs curry powder

1/2 cup heavy cream

salt and freshly ground pepper

Directions:

Sauté the onion and garlic together with the curry powder in a large saucepan. Stir in the parsnips and cook, stirring often, for 10 minutes. Add 6 cups of water, bring to the boil and simmer for 30 minutes or until the parsnips are tender.

Set aside to cool then blend in batches until smooth. Return soup to pan over low heat and stir in the cream. Do not boil - only heat through. Season with salt and pepper.

Pumpkin and Bell Pepper Soup

Serves 4

Ingredients:

1 medium leek, chopped

9 oz pumpkin, peeled, deseeded, cut into small cubes

1/2 red bell pepper, cut into small pieces

1 can tomatoes, undrained, crushed

2 cups vegetable broth

1/2 tsp ground cumin

salt and black pepper, to taste

Directions:

Heat the olive oil in a medium saucepan and sauté the leek for 4-5 minutes. Add the pumpkin and bell pepper and cook, stirring, for 2-3 minutes. Add tomatoes, broth and cumin and bring to the boil.

Cover, reduce heat to low and simmer, stirring occasionally, for 30 minutes or until vegetables are soft. Season with salt and pepper and leave aside to cool. Blend in batches and re-heat to serve.

Moroccan Pumpkin Soup

Serves 6

Ingredients :

1 leek, white part only, thinly sliced

3 cloves garlic, finely chopped

1/2 tsp ground ginger

1/2 tsp ground cinnamon

1/2 tsp ground cumin

2 carrots, peeled, coarsely chopped

2 lbs pumpkin, peeled, deseeded, diced

1/3 cup chick peas

5 tbsp olive oil

Juice of 1/2 lemon

parsley springs, to serve

Directions:

Heat oil in a large saucepan and sauté leek and garlic with 2 tsp salt, stirring occasionally, until soft. Add, cinnamon, ginger and cumin and stir again. Add carrots, pumpkin chick peas and 5 cups of water to saucepan and bring to the boil.

Reduce heat and simmer for 50 minutes or until chick peas are soft. Remove from heat, add lemon juice and blend soup, in batches, until smooth.

Return it to pan over low heat and cook, stirring, for 4 to 5 minutes or until heated through. Serve topped with parsley sprigs.

Spinach, Leek and Rice Soup

Serves 6

Ingredients:

2 leeks halved lengthwise and sliced

1 onion, chopped

2 garlic cloves, chopped

1/3 cup rice

1 can of diced tomatoes, undrained

2 cups of fresh spinach, cut

1 tbsp olive oil

4 cups vegetable broth

salt and pepper to taste

Directions:

Heat a large pot over medium heat. Add olive oil and onion and sauté for 2 minutes. Add leeks and cook for another 2-3 minutes, then add garlic and stir. Season with salt and pepper to taste.

Add the vegetable broth, canned tomatoes, and rice. Bring to a boil then reduce heat and simmer for about 10 minutes. Stir in spinach and cook for another 5 minutes.

Broccoli and Potato Soup

Serves 6

Ingredients:

2 lbs broccoli, cut into florets

2 potatoes, chopped

1 big onion, chopped

3 garlic cloves, crushed

4 cups water

1 tbsp olive oil

1/4 tsp ground nutmeg

Directions:

Heat oil in a large saucepan over medium-high heat. Add onion and garlic and sauté, stirring, for 3 minutes or until soft.

Add broccoli, potato and four cups of cold water. Cover and bring to the boil then reduce heat to low. Simmer, stirring, for 10 to 15 minutes or until potato is tender. Remove from heat. Blend until smooth.

Return to pan. Cook for five minutes or until heated through. Season with nutmeg and pepper before serving.

Leek, Rice and Potato Soup

Serves 6

Ingredients:

1 small onion, finely cut

2 leeks, halved lengthwise and sliced

2-3 potatoes, diced

1/3 cup rice

4 cups of water

3 tbsp sunflower oil

lemon juice, to serve

Directions:

Heat a soup pot over medium heat. Add sunflower oil and onion and sauté for 2 minutes. Add leeks and potatoes and stir for a few minutes more.

Add 4 cups of water, bring to a boil, reduce heat and simmer for 5 minutes. Add the very well washed rice and simmer for 10 minutes. Serve with lemon juice to taste.

Carrot and Chickpea Soup

Serves 4-5

Ingredients:

3-4 big carrots, chopped

1 leek, chopped

4 cups vegetable broth

1 cup canned chickpeas, undrained

1/2 cup orange juice

2 tbsp olive oil

1/2 tsp cumin

1/2 tsp ginger

4-5 tbsp yogurt, to serve

Directions:

Heat oil in a large saucepan over medium heat. Add leek and carrots and sauté until soft. Add orange juice, broth, chickpeas and spices. Bring to the boil.

Reduce heat to medium-low and simmer, covered, for 15 minutes. Blend soup until smooth, return to pan. Season with salt and pepper. Stir over heat until heated through. Pour in 4-5 bowls, top with yogurt and serve.

Spicy Carrot Soup

Serves 6-7

Ingredients:

10 carrots, peeled and chopped

2 medium onions, chopped

4-5 cups water

5 tbsp olive oil

2 cloves garlic, minced

1 red chili pepper, finely chopped

1/2 bunch, fresh coriander, finely cut

salt and pepper to taste

1/2 cup heavy cream

Directions:

Heat the olive oil in a large pot over medium heat, and sauté the onions, carrots, garlic and chili pepper until tender. Add 4-5 cups of water and bring to a boil. Reduce heat to low, and simmer 30 minutes.

Transfer the soup to a blender or food processor and blend until smooth. Return to the pot, and continue cooking for a few more minutes. Remove soup from heat, and stir in the cream. Serve with coriander sprinkled over each serving.

Lentil, Barley and Mushroom Soup

Serves 4

Ingredients*:*

2 medium leeks, trimmed, halved, sliced

10 white mushrooms, sliced

3 garlic cloves, cut

2 bay leaves

2 cans tomatoes, chopped, undrained

3/4 cup red lentils

1/3 cup barley

3 cups water

3 tbsp olive oil

1 tsp paprika

1 tsp savory

1/2 tsp cumin

Directions:

Heat oil in a large saucepan over medium-high heat. Sauté leeks and mushrooms for 3 to 4 minutes or until softened. Add cumin, paprika, savory and tomatoes, lentils, barley and 3 cups of cold water. Season with salt and pepper.

Cover and bring to the boil. Reduce heat to low. Simmer for 35 to 40 minutes or until barley is tender.

Creamy Mushroom Soup

Serves 4

Ingredients:

2 cups mushrooms, peeled and chopped

1 onion, chopped

2 cloves of garlic, crushed and chopped

1 tsp dried oregano

1 cup vegetable broth

salt and pepper to taste

3 tbsp sunflower or olive oil

Directions:

Sauté onions and garlic in a large soup pot until transparent. Add oregano and mushrooms.

Cook, stirring, for 10 minutes then add vegetable broth and simmer for another 10-20 minutes. Blend, season and serve.

Country French Vegetable Soup

Serves 6

Ingredients:

1 leek, thinly sliced

1 large zucchini, diced

1 cup green beans, cut

2 garlic cloves, cut

3 cups vegetable broth

1 can tomatoes, chopped

3.5 oz vermicelli, broken into small pieces

3 tbsp olive oil

black pepper to taste

4 tbsp freshly grated Parmesan cheese

Directions:

Heat olive oil in a large soup pot and sauté the leek, zucchini, green beans and garlic for about 5 minutes. Add the vegetable broth and stir in the tomatoes.

Bring to the boil, then reduce heat. Add black pepper to taste and simmer for 10 minutes or until the vegetables are tender, but still holding their shape. Stir in the vermicelli.

Cover again and simmer for 5 more minutes. Serve warm sprinkled with Parmesan cheese.

Simple Minted Pea Soup

Serves 4

Ingredients:

1 onion, finely chopped

2 garlic cloves, finely chopped

3 cups vegetable broth

1/3 cup mint leaves

2 lb green peas, frozen

3 tbsp sunflower oil

1/4 cup yogurt, to serve

small mint leaves, to serve

Directions:

Heat oil in a large saucepan over medium-high heat and sauté onion and garlic for 5 minutes or until soft.

Add vegetable broth and bring to the boil then add mint and peas. Cover, reduce heat and cook for 10 minutes or until peas are tender but still green.

Remove from heat. Set aside to cool slightly then blend soup, in batches, until smooth. Return soup to saucepan over medium-low heat and cook until heated through. Season with salt and pepper. Serve topped with yogurt, pepper and mint leaves.

Garden Minestrone

Serves 6-7

Ingredients:

1/4 cabbage, chopped

2 carrots, chopped

1 celery rib, thinly sliced

1 small onion, chopped

2 garlic cloves, chopped

2 tbsp olive oil

2 cups water

1 can tomatoes, diced, undrained

1 cup fresh spinach, torn

1/2 cup pasta, cooked

black pepper and salt to taste

Directions:

Sauté carrots, cabbage, celery, onion and garlic in oil for 5 minutes in a deep saucepan. Add water, tomatoes and bring to a boil.

Reduce heat and simmer uncovered, for 20 minutes or until vegetables are tender. Stir in spinach, pasta and season with pepper and salt to taste.

Potato Soup

Serves 8

Ingredients:

4-5 medium potatoes, peeled and cut into small cubes

2 carrots, chopped

1 zucchini, chopped

1 celery rib, chopped

3 cups water

3 tbsp olive oil

1 cup whole milk

1/2 tsp dried rosemary

salt to taste

black pepper to taste

a bunch of fresh parsley for garnish, finely cut

Directions:

Heat the olive oil over medium heat and sauté the vegetables for 2-3 minutes. Pour 3 cups of water, add the rosemary and bring the soup to a boil, then lower heat and simmer until all the vegetables are tender.

Blend soup in a blender until smooth. Add a cup of warm milk and blend some more. Serve warm , seasoned with black pepper and parsley sprinkled over each serving.

Cream of Cauliflower Soup

Serves 8

Ingredients:

1 large onion finely cut

1 medium head cauliflower, chopped

2-3 garlic cloves, minced

2 cups water

1/2 cup whole cream

4 tbsp olive oil

salt, to taste

fresh ground black pepper, to taste

Directions:

Heat the olive oil in a large pot over medium heat, and sauté the onion, cauliflower, garlic, Stir in the water, and bring the soup to a boil.

Reduce heat, cover, and simmer for 40 minutes. Remove the soup from heat add the cream and blend in a blender. Season with salt and pepper.

Roasted Red Pepper Soup

Serves 6-7

Ingredients:

5-6 red peppers

1 large onion, chopped

2 garlic cloves, crushed

4 medium tomatoes, chopped

2 cups vegetable broth

3 tbsp olive oil

2 bay leaves

Directions:

Grill the peppers or roast them in the oven at 480 F until the skins are a little burnt. Place the roasted peppers in a brown paper bag or a lidded container and leave covered for about 10 minutes. This makes it easier to peel them. Peel the skins and remove the seeds. Cut the peppers in small pieces.

Heat oil in a large saucepan over medium-high heat. Add onion and garlic and sauté, stirring, for 3 minutes or until onion has softened. Add the red peppers, bay leaves, tomato and simmer for 5 minutes.

Add broth. Season with pepper. Bring to the boil then reduce heat and simmer for 20 more minutes. Set aside to cool slightly. Blend, in batches, until smooth and serve.

Spinach Soup

Serves 6

Ingredients:

1 lb spinach, frozen

1 large onion or 4-5 spring onions

1 carrot

2 cups water

3-4 tbsp olive oil

1/4 cup white rice

1-2 cloves garlic, crushed

1 tsp paprika

black pepper

salt

Directions:

Chop the onion and spinach. Heat the oil in a cooking pot, add the onion and carrot and sauté together for a few minutes, until just softened. Add chopped garlic, paprika and rice and stir for a minute.

Remove from heat. Add the chopped spinach along with about 2 cups of hot water and season with salt and pepper. Bring back to a boil, then reduce the heat and simmer for around 15 minutes.

Spring Nettle Soup

Serves 6

Ingredients:

1.5 lb young top shoots of nettles, well washed

3-4 tbsp sunflower oil

2 potatoes, diced small

1 bunch spring onions, coarsely chopped

2 cups freshly boiled water

1 tsp salt

Directions:

Clean the young nettles, wash and cook them in slightly salted water. Drain, rinse, drain again and then chop or pass through a sieve.

Sauté the chopped spring onions and potatoes in the oil until the potatoes start to color a little. Turn off the heat, add the nettles, then gradually stir in the water. Stir well, then simmer until the potatoes are cooked through.

Gazpacho

Serves 6-7

Ingredients:

2.25 lb tomatoes, peeled and halved

1 onion, sliced

1 green pepper, sliced

1 big cucumber, peeled and sliced

2 cloves garlic

salt to taste

4 tbsp olive oil

1 tbsp apple cider vinegar

to garnish

1/2 onion, chopped

1 green pepper, chopped

1 cucumber, chopped

Directions:

Place the tomatoes, garlic, onion, green pepper, cucumber, salt, olive oil and vinegar in a blender or food processor and puree until smooth, adding small amounts of cold water if needed to achieve desired consistency.

Serve gazpacho chilled with the chopped onion, green pepper and cucumber.

Cold Cucumber Soup

Serves 6

Ingredients:

1 large or two small cucumbers

2 cups yogurt

4-5 cloves garlic, crushed or chopped

1 cup cold water

4 tbsp sunflower or olive oil

2 bunches of fresh dill, finely chopped

1/2 cup crushed walnuts

Directions:

Wash the cucumber, peel and cut into small cubes. In a large bowl dilute the yogurt with water to taste, add the cucumber and garlic stirring well.

Add salt to the taste, garnish with the dill and the crushed walnuts and put in the fridge to cool.

Main Dishes

Zucchini Bake

Serves 4

Ingredients:

5 medium zucchinis, grated

1 carrot, grated

1 small tomato, diced

1 onion, halved, thinly sliced

2 garlic cloves, crushed

1 cup self-raising flour, sifted

5 eggs, lightly whisked

1/2 cup sunflower oil

1/2 cup fresh dill, finely cut

1 cup grated feta cheese

2 cups yogurt, to serve (optional)

Directions:

Preheat oven to 350 F. Grease and line a round, 8 inch base, baking dish. Combine zucchinis, carrot, tomato, onion, garlic and dill in a bowl. Add flour, eggs, oil and cheese. Season and stir until well combined.

Bake for 30-40 minutes. Serve with yogurt.

Eggplant Stew

Serves 4

Ingredients:

2 medium eggplants, peeled and diced

1 cup canned tomatoes, drained and diced

1 zucchini, diced

9-10 black olives, pitted

1 onion, chopped

4 garlic cloves, chopped

2 tbsp tomato paste

1 cup canned tomatoes, drained and diced

1 bunch of parsley, chopped, to serve

3 tbsp olive oil

½ tsp paprika

salt and black pepper, to taste

Directions:

Gently sauté onions, garlic, and eggplants in olive oil on medium-high heat for 10 minutes. Add paprika and tomato paste and stir for 1-2 minutes. Add in the rest of the ingredients.

Cover and simmer on low-heat for 30 40 minutes. Sprinkle with parsley and serve.

Zucchini Fritters

Serves 4

Ingredients:

5-6 zucchinis, grated

3 eggs

1/2 cup fresh dill, finely cut

1 tsp fresh mint, chopped

3 garlic cloves, crushed

5-6 spring onions, very finely chopped

1 cup feta cheese, crumbled

salt and black pepper, to taste

1 cup flour

1/2 cup sunflower oil, for frying

Directions:

Grate zucchinis and put them in a colander. Sprinkle with salt set aside to drain for 15 minutes. Squeeze and place in a bowl. Add all the other ingredients except for flour and the sunflower oil. Stir very well. Add in flour and mix again.

Heat the sunflower oil in a frying pan. Drop a few scoops of the zucchini mixture and fry them on medium heat, making sure they don't touch. Fry for 3-5 minutes, until golden brown. Serve with yogurt.

Spinach with Eggs

Serves 2

Ingredients:

1 lb spinach, fresh or frozen

1 onion, finely cut

4 eggs

3 tbsp olive oil

1/4 tsp cumin

1 tsp paprika

salt and pepper, to taste

Directions:

Heat olive oil on medium-low heat in a skillet. Gently sauté onion for 3-4 minutes. Add paprika and cumin and stir. Add spinach and sauté some more until it wilts. Season with salt and black pepper to taste.

Prepare 4 holes on the spinach bed for the eggs. Break an egg into each hole. Cover and cook until eggs are cooked through. Serve with bread and a dollop of yogurt.

Artichoke and Onion Frittata

Serves 4

Ingredients:

1 small onion, chopped

1 cup marinated artichoke hearts, drained

6 eggs

1 garlic clove, crushed

1 tbsp olive oil

salt and freshly ground black pepper

1/2 bunch fresh parsley, finely cut, to serve

Directions:

Heat oil in a non-stick oven pan over medium heat and sauté onion stirring occasionally, for 5-6 minutes or until golden brown. Add artichokes and cook for 2 minutes or until heated through.

Whisk eggs with garlic until combined well. Season with salt and pepper. Pour the egg mixture over the artichoke mixture. Reduce heat, cover and cook for 10 minutes or until frittata is set around the edge but still runny in the center.

Place pan into preheated oven and cook 4-5 until golden brown. Remove from oven and cut into wedges. Serve sprinkled with parsley.

Feta Cheese Stuffed Zucchinis

Serves 5-6

Ingredients:

5-6 zucchinis

3.5 oz feta cheese, grated

3 eggs

1 onion, finely chopped

1/2 cup milk

3.5 oz butter

salt

Directions:

Halve the peeled zucchinis lengthwise, hollow and salt. Sauté the finely chopped onion in half of the butter. Combine half of the milk, grated feta cheese and 1 egg in a bowl.

Stuff the zucchinis with the mixture, arrange in a baking dish and pour over the remaining 2 eggs beaten with the rest of the milk.

Bake for approximately 30 min in a preheated oven. A few minutes before the dish is ready fleck the remaining butter over the zucchinis.

Zucchini and Almond Pasta

Serves 4

Ingredients:

2 cups fusilli (or other short pasta)

1 tbsp olive oil

2 garlic cloves, crushed

4 zucchinis, coarsely grated

1/2 cup slivered almonds, lightly toasted

2 tbs chopped fresh parsley

1 tbs chopped mint leaves

2 tbs grated Parmesan cheese

Directions:

Cook the pasta according to package instructions until al dente.

Heat oil in a large frying pan over medium heat and sauté the garlic and for 30 seconds. Add the zucchinis and sauté, stirring occasionally, for 5 minutes or until all the liquid has evaporated. Add almonds and herbs, stir to combine and season with salt and pepper.

Drain the cooked pasta, add to the pan together with the Parmesan and toss to combine.

Poached Eggs with Feta and Yogurt

Serves 4

Ingredients:

12 eggs

2 cups plain yogurt

10 oz feta cheese, shredded

2 tsp paprika

3 cloves garlic

2 oz butter

Directions:

Crush the garlic and stir together with the yogurt and the grated cheese. Divide the mixture into four plates.

Poach the eggs, take them out with a serving spoon and place three eggs on top of the mixture in each plate.

Brown the butter together with the paprika and pour one quarter over each plate before serving.

Mish-Mash

Serves 5-6

Ingredients:

2 small onions, chopped

1 green bell pepper, chopped

2 red bell peppers, chopped

4 tomatoes, cubed

2 garlic cloves, crushed

8 eggs

9 oz feta cheese, crumbled

4 tbsp olive oil

half a bunch parsley

black pepper

salt

Directions:

In a large pan sauté onions over medium heat, till transparent. Reduce heat and add bell peppers and garlic. Continue cooking until soft.

Add the tomatoes and continue simmering until the mixture is almost dry. Add the cheese and all eggs and cook until well mixed and not too liquid.

Season with black pepper and remove from the heat. Sprinkle with parsley.

Eggs and Feta Cheese Stuffed Peppers

Serves 4

Ingredients:

8 red bell peppers

6 eggs

4 oz feta cheese

a bunch of parsley

2 cups breadcrumbs

sunflower oil

Directions:

Grill the peppers or roast them in the oven at 480 F. Peel and deseed the peppers. Mix the crumbled feta cheese with 4 beaten eggs.

Stuff the peppers with the feta mixture. Beat the remaining two eggs. Roll each stuffed pepper first in breadcrumbs then dip in the beaten eggs.

Fry in hot oil turning once. Serve sprinkled with parsley.

Feta Cheese Baked in Foil

Serves 4

Ingredients:

14 oz hard feta cheese

3 oz butter

1 tbsp paprika

1 tsp savory

Directions:

Cut the feta cheese into four medium-thick slices and place on sheets of butter-lined foil.

Place cubes of butter on top each feta cheese piece, sprinkle with paprika and savory and wrap. Place in a tray and bake in a moderate oven. Serve wrapped in the foil.

Breaded Cheese

Serves 4

Ingredients:

14 oz feta cheese

2 eggs, beaten

2 tbsp flour

3-4 tbsp breadcrumbs

vegetable oil for frying

Directions:

Cut the cheese in four equal slices. Dip each piece first in cold water, then roll in the flour, then in the beaten eggs, and finally in the breadcrumbs.

Fry these cheese pieces in preheated oil on both sides. Serve warm.

Bulgarian Baked Beans

Serves 6

Ingredients:

2 cups dried white beans

2 medium onions, chopped

1 red bell pepper, chopped

1 carrot, chopped

1/4 cup sunflower oil

1 tsp paprika

1 tsp black pepper

1 tbsp plain flour

1/2 bunch fresh parsley and mint

1 tsp salt

Directions:

Wash the beans and soak in water overnight. In the morning discard the water, pour enough cold water to cover the beans, add one of the onions, peeled but left whole. Cook until the beans are soft but not falling apart. If there is too much water left, drain the beans.

Chop the other onion and fry it a frying pan along with the chopped bell pepper and the carrot. Add paprika, plain flour and the beans. Stir well and pour the mixture in a baking dish along with some parsley, mint, and salt. Bake in a preheated to 350 F oven for 20 to 30 minutes. The beans should not be too dry. Serve warm.

Rice Stuffed Bell Peppers

Serves 4

Ingredients:

8 bell peppers, cored and seeded

1 1/2 cups rice, washed and drained

2 onions, chopped

1 tomato, chopped

fresh parsley, chopped

3 tbsp oil

1 tbsp paprika

Directions:

Heat the oil and sauté the onions for 2-3 minutes. Add the paprika, the washed and rinsed rice, the tomato, and season with salt and pepper. Add 1/2 cup of hot water and cook the rice until the water is absorbed.

Stuff each pepper with the mixture using a spoon. Every pepper should be 3/4 full. Arrange the peppers in a deep oven proof dish and top up with warm water to half fill the dish.

Cover and bake for about 30 minutes at 350 F. Uncover and cook for another 10 minutes until the peppers are well cooked. Serve on their own or with plain yogurt.

Bean Stuffed Bell Peppers

Serves 5

Ingredients:

10 dried red bell peppers

1 cup dried beans

1 onion

3 cloves garlic

2 tbsp flour

1 carrot

1 bunch of parsley

1/2 crushed walnuts

1 tsp paprika

salt

Directions:

Put the dried peppers in warm water and leave them for 1 hour.

Cook the beans.

Chop the carrot and the onion, sauté them and add them to the cooked beans. Add as well the finely chopped parsley and the walnuts. Stir the mixture to make it homogeneous.

Drain the peppers, then fill them with the mixture and place in a roasting tin, covering the peppers` openings with flour to seal them during the baking. Bake it for about 30 min. at 350 F.

Monastery Stew

Serves 4

Ingredients:

3-4 potatoes, diced

2-3 tomatoes, diced

1-2 carrots, chopped

1-2 onions, finely chopped

1 cup small shallots, whole

1 celery rib, chopped

2 cups fresh mushrooms, chopped

1/2 cup black olives, pitted

1/4 cup rice

1/3 cup white wine

1/3 cup sunflower oil

1 bunch of parsley

1 tsp black pepper

1 tsp salt

Directions:

Sauté the finely chopped onions, carrots and celery in a little oil. Add the small onions, olives, mushrooms and black pepper and stir well. Pour over the wine and 1 cup of water, salt, cover and let simmer until tender.

After 15 minutes add the diced potatoes, the rice, and the tomato pieces. Transfer everything into a clay pot, sprinkle with parsley and bake for about 30 minutes at 350 F.

Potato and Leek Stew

Serves 4

Ingredients:

3-4 potatoes

2-3 leek stems cut into thick rings

5-6 tbsp olive oil

1/2 bunch of parsley

1/2 cup grated yellow cheese (cheddar or Gruyère)

salt

Directions:

Peel the potatoes, wash them and cut them into small cubes. Slice the leeks. Put the potatoes and the leeks in a pot along with some water and the oil. The water should cover the vegetables.

Season with salt and bring to the boil then simmer until tender. Sprinkle with the finely chopped parsley and the grated yellow cheese.

Spinach with Rice

Serves 4

Ingredients:

3-4 cups fresh spinach, washed, drained and chopped

1/2 cup of rice

1 onion, chopped

1 carrot, chopped

1/4 cup olive oil

2 cups water

Directions:

Heat the oil in a large skillet and cook the onions and the carrot until soft, add the paprika and the washed and drained rice and mix well. Add two cups of warm water stirring constantly as the rice absorbs it, and simmer for 10 more minutes.

Wash the spinach well and cut it in strips then add to the rice and cook until it wilts. Remove from the heat and season to taste. Serve with yogurt.

Stewed Green Beans

Serves 5-6

Ingredients:

2 lb green beans, fresh or frozen

2 onions, chopped

4 cloves garlic, crushed

1/2 cup sunflower oil

1 bunch fresh parsley, chopped

1 bunch of fresh dill, finely chopped

2 potatoes, peeled and cut in small chunks

2 carrots, sliced

1 cup water

2 tbsp salt

pepper to taste

Directions:

Sauté the onions and the garlic lightly in olive oil. Add the green beans, and the remaining ingredients.

Cover and simmer over medium heat for about an hour or until all vegetables are tender. Check after 30 minutes; add more water if necessary. Serve warm - sprinkled with the fresh dill.

Cabbage and Rice Stew

Serves 4

Ingredients:

1 cup long grain white rice

2 cups water

2 tbsp olive oil

1 small onion, chopped

1 clove garlic, crushed

1/4 head cabbage, cored and shredded

2 tomatoes, diced

1 tbsp paprika

1/2 bunch of parsley

salt to taste

black pepper to taste

Directions:

Heat the olive oil in a large pot. Add the onion and garlic and cook until transparent. Add the paprika, rice and water, stir and bring to boil.

Simmer for 10 minutes. Add the shredded cabbage, the tomatoes, and cook for about 20 minutes, stirring occasionally, until the cabbage cooks down. Season with salt and pepper and serve sprinkled with parsley.

Potatoes Baked in Milk

Serves 5-6

Ingredients:

4-5 medium potatoes

1 cup milk

5 tbsp olive oil

1 tsp salt

1 tsp black pepper

1 tsp paprika

1 tsp savory

Directions:

Wash the potatoes, peel them and cut them in thin slices. Put in a large baking dish together with the milk, oil, salt, pepper, paprika and savory.

Combine everything very well. Bake for about 30 minutes at 350 F.

New Potatoes with Herbs

Serves 4-5

Ingredients:

2 lb small new potatoes

1 tbsp dried peppermint

2 oz butter

1 tbsp finely chopped parsley

1 tbsp dried rosemary

1 tbsp dried oregano

1 tbsp dill

1 tsp salt

1 tsp black pepper

Directions:

Wash the young potatoes, cut them in halves if too big, and put them in a baking dish.

Melt the butter and pour over the potatoes. Season with the herbs, salt and pepper. Bake for 30-40 minutes at 350 F

Breakfasts and Desserts

Berry Quinoa Breakfast

Serves 2

Ingredients:

½ cup quinoa

1 cup milk

¼ cup fresh blueberries or raspberries

1 tbsp walnuts or almonds, chopped

Directions:

Wash quinoa and cook according to package directions. Combine it with milk in and bring to a boil.

Cover, reduce heat and simmer for 15 minutes. When ready add walnuts and cinnamon, place a portion of the quinoa into a bowl and top with fresh blueberries.

Cherry Quinoa Cookies

Serves 10-12

Ingredients:

1 cup cooked quinoa

1 cup whole wheat white flour

4 tbsp unsalted butter, melted

¼ cup honey

¼ cup sugar

½ cup dried cherries

boiling water

½ tsp baking powder

½ tsp salt

1 egg

1 tsp vanilla extract

½ cup sliced almonds or walnuts

Directions:

Soak dried cherries in boiling water for 10 minutes. In a medium bowl, whisk together flour, baking powder, and salt. In a large bowl, whisk together butter, honey, and brown sugar until well combined and lightened in color. Whisk in the egg. Add vanilla extract and whisk again. Stir in flour mixture, quinoa, almonds, and cherries until well combined. Cover dough and let "sit"for half an hour.

Preheat oven to 350 F. Line two baking sheets with baking paper. Place a teaspoon of cookie dough into the palm of your hand. Roll the cookie dough between your palms until it retains a spherical shape.

Align every cookie dough about 2 inch from the previous. Bake cookies until golden, about 12 minutes.

Quinoa Chocolate Chip Cookies

Serves 10

Ingredients:

1 cup quinoa flakes

1 cup flour

½ cup of melted butter

½ cup sugar

1 egg

½ tsp baking powder

½ tsp salt

1 tsp vanilla powder

5.5 oz chocolate chips

Directions:

Cream butter and sugar together. Add eggs and vanilla and combine. Mix dry ingredients together separately then slowly add to the butter mixture. Add the chocolate chips.

Preheat oven to 350 F. Line two baking sheets with baking paper. Place a teaspoon of cookie dough into the palm of your hand. Roll the cookie dough between your palms until it retains a spherical shape.

Align every cookie dough about 2 inch from the previous. Bake cookies until golden, about 12 minutes.

Tahini Quinoa Cookies

Serves 8-10

Ingredients:

1 cup rice flour

1 cup quinoa

½ cup honey

1/3 cup brown sugar

½ cup butter

½ cup tahini

1 tsp baking soda

¼ tsp salt

½ teaspoon vanilla

Directions:

Preheat oven to 350 F degrees. Combine sugar, honey, tahini and butter stirring until creamy. Add remaining ingredients. Mix well.

Spoon rounded teaspoonfuls of dough onto cookie sheets. Bake for 10-12 minutes, or until cookies start to turn golden brown.

Quinoa and Banana Muffins

Serves 12

Ingredients:

2/3 cups flour

½ cup quinoa

2 ripe bananas, mashed

¼ cup sugar

½ cup milk

1 egg

3 tbsp sunflower oil

1 tsp vanilla

1 tbsp baking powder

½ tsp cinnamon

½ tsp salt

Directions:

Preheat oven to 350 F. Combine wet ingredients and mix well. In a separate bowl mix dry ingredients.

Add dry ingredients to wet ingredients gently stirring.

Grease or line 12 muffin tins. Spoon dough evenly into cups.

Bake for 15 minutes or until a toothpick comes out clean.

Strawberry Jam Crêpes

Serves 10

Ingredients:

3 eggs

1/4 cup sugar

2 cups plain flour

2 cups milk

1 large orange, juiced

1/2 tsp vanilla

1/4 cup sunflower oil

1/2 cup strawberry jam

Directions:

Using an electric mixer, lightly beat eggs and 1/4 cup sugar on medium speed until well combined. Add 1/2 cup flour, 1 tablespoon at a time, beating well after each addition. Slowly add remaining 1 1/2 cups flour and milk alternately until batter is smooth. Reduce mixer speed to medium low. Add 1/2 cup orange juice, vanilla and a pinch of salt. Beat until batter is smooth.

Heat a 7 inch base crêpe pan or frying pan over medium heat. Brush pan with a little oil. Pour 2 1/2 tbsp batter into center of pan and swirl to coat base. Cook for 1 to 2 minutes or until base is golden. Turn and cook for 30 seconds. Transfer to a plate. Repeat with remaining batter, greasing pan between crêpes.

Spread 1 tsp jam over 1 crêpe. Roll crêpe up tightly. Repeat with remaining crêpes and jam. Layer crêpes on a serving plate. Serve sprinkled with powdered sugar.

French Toast

Serves 4

Ingredients:

8 slices stale bread

4 eggs, beaten

2/3 cup milk

1/2 cup sunflower oil

Directions:

Slice the bread into thin 1/2 inch slices. Dip first in milk, then in the beaten eggs.

Fry in hot oil. Serve hot, sprinkled with sugar, honey, jam, feta cheese or whatever topping you prefer.

Quick Peach Tarts

Serves 4

Ingredients:

1 sheet frozen ready-rolled puff pastry

1/4 cup light cream cheese spread

1 1/2 tablespoons raw sugar

pinch of cinnamon

4 peaches, peeled, halved, stones removed, sliced

Directions:

Preheat oven to 350 F. Line a baking tray with non-stick baking paper. Cut pastry into 4 squares. Place onto prepared tray.

Using a spoon, mix cream cheese, one tablespoon of sugar, vanilla and cinnamon. Spread over pastry squares. Arrange peach slices over top.

Bake for 10 minutes or until golden. Sprinkle with remaining sugar and serve.

Baked Apples

Serves 4

Ingredients:

8 medium sized apples

1/3 cup walnuts, crushed

3/4 cup sugar

3 tbsp raisins, soaked

vanilla, cinnamon according to taste

2 oz butter.

Directions:

Peel and carefully hollow the apples. Prepare stuffing by beating butter, 3/4 cup of sugar, crushed walnuts, raisins and cinnamon.

Stuff the apples and place in an oiled dish, pour over 1-2 tbsp of water and bake in a moderate oven. Serve warm with a scoop of vanilla ice cream.

Cherry Clafoutis

Serves 4

Ingredients:

1/2 cup all-purpose flour

1/4 cup plus 2 tablespoons sugar

pinch of salt

3 large eggs

3 tbsp unsalted butter, melted

zest of 1 lemon

1/4 cup plus 2 tbsp milk

3 cups cherries

1 tbsp Cognac or brandy (optional)

1 tsp vanilla

powder sugar, for dusting

Directions:

Pit the cherries using a cherry pitter. Place the cherries on a small tray in a single layer, scatter with 1/4 cup sugar and shake gently to coat in sugar. Place in the freezer for 1 hour or until firm.

Preheat the oven to 350 F. Butter a 9-inch gratin dish. In a bowl, whisk the flour, sugar, vanilla and a pinch of salt. Whisk in the eggs, butter, brandy and lemon zest until smooth. Add the milk and whisk until light and very smooth, about 3 minutes. Pour the batter into the dish and top with the cherries.

Bake for about 30 minutes, until the clafoutis is set and golden. Let cool slightly. Dust with powder sugar.

Pumpkin Pastry

Serves 8

Ingredients:

14 oz filo pastry

1 cups pumpkin, shredded

1 cup walnuts, coarsely chopped

1/2 cup sugar

6 tbsp oil

1 tbsp cinnamon

1 tsp vanilla powder

Directions:

Grate the pumpkin and steam it until tender. Cool and add the walnuts, sugar, cinnamon and the vanilla.

Place two sheets of pastry in the baking dish, sprinkle with oil and spread the filling on top. Repeat this a few times finishing with a sheet of pastry.

Bake for 20 minutes at 350 F. Let the Pumpkin Pie cool down and dust with the powder sugar.

Sweet Cheese Balls in Syrup

Serves 6

Ingredients:

3.5 oz feta or cottage cheese

3 eggs

1 cup flour

1 tsp baking soda

1 cup sunflower oil

For the syrup: 3 cups water, 3/2 cup sugar, vanilla

Directions:

Mix the feta cheese and eggs well, before gradually adding the flour, followed by the baking soda.

Shape into balls with a spoon and fry in hot oil until golden-brown. When cooled, pour over syrup made from water, sugar and vanilla.

Bulgarian Cake

Serves 12 (24 pieces)

Ingredients:

3 eggs, beaten

1 cup sugar

1 cup yogurt

1/2 cup vegetable oil

1 tbsp baking powder

1 tbsp vanilla

1 tsp grated fresh lemon rind

1 tablespoon cocoa

3 cups plain flour

Directions:

Beat eggs with the sugar and add the vegetable oil. Add yogurt. Mix the baking powder with the flour and add to the eggs along with vanilla and lemon rind.

Preheat oven to 350 F. Warm a 10 inch diameter round cake tin in the oven. Pour two thirds of the mixture into the warm cake tin. Add a tablespoon of cocoa to the remaining dough, mix well and pour in the cake tin. Bake for about 35 minutes.

Oatmeal Muffins

Serves 6

Ingredients:

1 cup rolled oats

1 cup flour

1/2 cup sugar

1/2 tsp of salt

1 tsp baking powder

1/2 tsp baking soda

1/2 tsp of cinnamon

1/4 cup walnuts, crushed

1/3 cup of raisins

1/2 cup butter, melted and cooled

1 cup buttermilk

1 tsp lemon zest

1 tsp vanilla extract

1 large egg, beaten

Directions:

Preheat the oven to 350 F and grease a twelve-hole muffin tin.

Mix together the rolled oats, sugar, flour, salt, baking soda, baking powder, cinnamon, walnuts and raisins. In a separate bowl mix together the butter, buttermilk, egg, vanilla and lemon zest.

Pour the wet ingredients into the dry mixture and stir for about 15 seconds, just to bring the ingredients together. Scoop into muffin tin and bake for 15 minutes or until a toothpick comes out clean. Set aside for a minute or two and transfer to a wire rack to cool completely.

Chocolate Peanut Butter Melts

Serves 24

Ingredients:

1 1/2 sheets frozen ready-rolled shortcrust pastry

1/2 cup smooth peanut butter

24 chocolate melts

Directions:

Preheat oven to 350 F. Grease two 12 hole mini muffin pans. Using a small cup cut 24 rounds from pastry sheets. Press rounds into prepared pan holes. Spoon 1 tsp peanut butter into each pastry case.

Bake for 8 minutes or until pastry is golden. Top each tart with one chocolate melt. Bake for two minutes or until chocolate has melted. Transfer to a wire rack to cool slightly and serve.

Bulgarian Rice Pudding

Serves 4

Ingredients:

1 cup short-grain white rice

6 tbsp sugar

1 1/2 cup water

1 1/2 cup whole milk

1 cinnamon stick

1 strip lemon zest

Directions:

Place the rice in a saucepan, cover with water and cook over low heat for about 15 minutes.

Add milk, sugar, cinnamon stick and lemon zest and cook over very low heat, stirring frequently until the mixture is creamy. Do not let it boil.

When ready discard cinnamon stick and lemon zest. Serve warm or at room temperature.

Baklava-Walnut Pie

Serves: 15

Ingredients:

14 oz filo pastry

1 cup ground walnuts

9 oz butter

For the syrup:

2 cups sugar

2 cups water

1 tbsp vanilla powder

2 tbsp lemon zest

Directions:

Grease a baking tray and place 2-3 sheets of pastry. Crush the walnuts and spread some evenly on the pastry. Place two more sheets of the filo pastry on top. Repeat until all the pastry sheets and walnuts have been used up. Always finish with some sheets of pastry on top.

Cut the pie in the tray into small squares. Melt the butter and pour it over the pie. Bake in a preheated oven at 350 F until light brown. When ready set aside to cool.

The syrup: Combine water and sugar in a saucepan. Add vanilla and lemon zest and bring to the boil, then lower the heat and simmer for about 5 minutes until the syrup is nearly thick.

Pour hot syrup over the cold baked pie. Leave to stand for at least 1-2 days until completely dry.

FREE BONUS RECIPES: 10 Ridiculously Easy Jam and Jelly Recipes Anyone Can Make

A Different Strawberry Jam

Makes 6-7 11 oz jars

Ingredients:

4 lb fresh small strawberries (stemmed and cleaned)

5 cups sugar

1 cup water

2 tbsp lemon juice or 1 tsp citric acid

Directions:

Mix water and sugar and bring to the boil. Simmer sugar syrup for 5-6 minutes then slowly drop in the cleaned strawberries. Stir and bring to the boil again. Lower heat and simmer, stirring and skimming any foam off the top once or twice.

Drop a small amount of the jam on a plate and wait a minute to see if it has thickened. If it has gelled enough, turn off the heat. If not, keep boiling and test every 5 minutes until ready. Two or three minutes before you remove the jam from the heat, add lemon juice or citric acid and stir well.

Ladle the hot jam in the jars until 1/8-inch from the top. Place the lid on top and flip the jar upside down. Continue until all of the jars are filled and upside down. Allow the jam to cool completely before turning right-side up. Press on the lid to check and see if it has sealed. If one of the jars lids doesn't pop up- the jar is not sealed–store it in a refrigerator.

Raspberry Jam

Makes 4-5 11 oz jars

Ingredients:

4 cups raspberries

4 cups sugar

1 tsp vanilla extract

1/2 tsp citric acid

Directions:

Gently wash and drain the raspberries. Lightly crush them with a potato masher, food mill or a food processor. Do not puree, it is better to have bits of fruit. Sieve half of the raspberry pulp to remove some of the seeds.

Combine sugar and raspberries in a wide, thick-bottomed pot and bring mixture to a full rolling boil, stirring constantly. Skim any scum or foam that rises to the surface. Boil until the jam sets.

Test by putting a small drop on a cold plate – if the jam is set, it will wrinkle when given a small poke with your finger. Add citric acid, vanilla, and stir. Simmer for 2-3 minutes more, then ladle into hot jars. Flip upside down or process 10 minutes in boiling water.

Raspberry-Peach Jam

Makes 4-5 11 oz jars

Ingredients:

2 lb peaches

1 1/2 cup raspberries

4 cups sugar

1 tsp citric acid

Directions:

Wash and slice the peaches. Clean the raspberries and combine them with the peaches is a wide, heavy-bottomed saucepan. Cover with sugar and set aside for a few hours or overnight.

Bring the fruit and sugar to a boil over medium heat, stirring occasionally. Remove any foam that rises to the surface.

Boil until the jam sets. Add citric acid and stir. Simmer for 2-3 minutes more, then ladle into hot jars. Flip upside down or process 10 minutes in boiling water.

Blueberry Jam

Makes 4-5 11 oz jars

Ingredients:

4 cups granulated sugar

3 cups blueberries (frozen and thawed or fresh)

3/4 cup honey

2 tbsp lemon juice

1 tsp lemon zest

Directions:

Gently wash and drain the blueberries. Lightly crush them with a potato masher, food mill or a food processor. Add the honey, lemon juice, and lemon zest, then bring to a boil over medium-high heat. Boil for 10-15 minutes, stirring from time to time. Boil until the jam sets.

Test by putting a small drop on a cold plate – if the jam is set, it will wrinkle when given a small poke with your finger. Skim off any foam, then ladle the jam into jars. Seal, flip upside down or process for 10 minutes in boiling water.

Triple Berry Jam

Makes 4-5 11 oz jars

Ingredients:

1 cup strawberries

1 cup raspberries

2 cups blueberries

4 cups sugar

1 tsp citric acid

Directions:

Mix berries and add sugar. Set aside for a few hours or overnight. Bring the fruit and sugar to the boil over medium heat, stirring frequently. Remove any foam that rises to the surface. Boil until the jam sets. Add citric acid, salt and stir.

Simmer for 2-3 minutes more, then ladle into hot jars. Flip upside down or process 10 minutes in boiling water.

Red Currant Jelly

Makes 6-7 11 oz jars

Ingredients:

2 lb fresh red currants

1/2 cup water

3 cups sugar

1 tsp citric acid

Directions:

Place the currants into a large pot, and crush with a potato masher or berry crusher. Add in water, and bring to a boil. Simmer for 10 minutes. Strain the fruit through a jelly or cheese cloth and measure out 4 cups of the juice.

Pour the juice into a large saucepan, and stir in the sugar. Bring to full rolling boil, then simmer for 20-30 minutes, removing any foam that may rise to the surface. When the jelly sets, ladle in hot jars, flip upside down or process in boiling water for 10 minutes.

White Cherry Jam

Makes 3-4 11 oz jars

Ingredients:

2 lb cherries

3 cups sugar

2 cups water

1 tsp citric acid

Directions:

Wash and stone cherries. Combine water and sugar and bring to the boil. Boil for 5-6 minutes then remove from heat and add cherries. Bring to a rolling boil and cook until set. Add citric acid, stir and boil 1-2 minutes more.

Ladle in hot jars, flip upside down or process in boiling water for 10 minutes.

Cherry Jam

Makes 3-4 11 oz jars

Ingredients:

2 lb fresh cherries, pitted, halved

4 cups sugar

1/2 cup lemon juice

Directions:

Place the cherries in a large saucepan. Add sugar and set aside for an hour. Add the lemon juice and place over low heat.

Cook, stirring occasionally, for 10 minutes or until sugar dissolves. Increase heat to high and bring to a rolling boil.

Cook for 5-6 minutes or until jam is set. Remove from heat and ladle hot jam into jars, seal and flip upside down.

Oven Baked Ripe Figs Jam

Makes 3-4 11 oz jars

Ingredients:

2 lb ripe figs

2 cups sugar

1 ½ cups water

2 tbsp lemon juice

Directions:

Arrange the figs in a Dutch oven, if they are very big, cut them in halves. Add sugar and water and stir well. Bake at 350 F for about one and a half hours. Do not stir. You can check the readiness by dropping a drop of the syrup in a cup of cold water – if it falls to the bottom without dissolving, the jam is ready. If the drop dissolves before falling, you can bake it a little longer.

Take out of the oven, add lemon juice and ladle in the warm jars. Place the lids on top and flip the jars upside down. Allow the jam to cool completely before turning right-side up.

If you want to process the jams - place them into a large pot, cover the jars with water by at least 2 inches and bring to a boil. Boil for 10 minutes, remove the jars and sit to cool.

Quince Jam

Makes 5-6 11 oz jars

Ingredients:

4 lb quinces

5 cups sugar

2 cups water

1 tsp lemon zest

3 tbsp lemon juice

Directions:

Combine water and sugar in a deep, thick-bottomed saucepan and bring it to the boil. Simmer, stirring until the sugar has completely dissolved. Rinse the quinces, cut in half, and discard the cores. Grate the quinces, using a cheese grater or a blender to make it faster. Quince flesh tends to darken very quickly, so it is good to do this as fast as possible.

Add the grated quinces to the sugar syrup and cook uncovered, stirring occasionally until the jam turns pink and thickens to desired consistency, about 40 minutes.

Drop a small amount of the jam on a plate and wait a minute to see if it has thickened. If it has gelled enough, turn off the heat. If not, keep boiling and test every 2-3 minutes until ready. Two or three minutes before you remove the jam from the heat, add lemon juice and lemon zest and stir well.

Ladle in hot, sterilized jars and flip upside down.

About the Author

Vesela lives in Bulgaria with her family of six (including the Jack Russell Terrier). Her passion is going green in everyday life and she loves to prepare homemade cosmetic and beauty products for all her family and friends.

Vesela has been publishing her cookbooks for over a year now. If you want to see other healthy family recipes that she has published, together with some natural beauty books, you can check out her Author Page on Amazon.

Made in the USA
San Bernardino, CA
14 May 2017